# How to
# WIN
at
# GYMKHANAS

# How to
# WIN
at
# GYMKHANAS

TONI WEBBER

ASHFORD
Southampton

Published by Ashford
      1 Church Road
      Shedfield
      Hampshire
      SO3 2HW

Whilst great care has been taken in the compilation of this book, it is regretted that neither author nor publisher can accept responsibility for the use, or consequences of the use, of the information and advice contained herein.

*British Library Cataloguing in Publication Data*

Webber, Toni
  How to win at gymkhanas.
  1. Gymkhanas – Amateurs' manuals
  I. Title
  798.2'4

ISBN 1-85253-129-0

Cartoons and illustrations by Dave Stephens
Typeset by Staples Printers Rochester Limited,
Love Lane, Rochester, Kent.
Printed in Great Britain.

# Contents

INTRODUCTION                                vii
1. THE GYMKHANA PONY                         1
2. TRAINING TIPS FOR PONY
   AND RIDER                                 14
3. GYMKHANA EVENTS                           39
4. PRACTISING RINGCRAFT                      66
5. TIPS ON TEAMWORK                          72
6. EQUIPMENT FOR PRACTISING                  82
7. DRESS AND SADDLERY                        97
8. THE DAY OF THE SHOW                      107
   USEFUL ADDRESSES                         118

For all members of the Southdown Hunt
East Mounted Games Squad in the
hope – and belief – that, sooner or later,
they will qualify for Wembley

# Introduction

Gymkhanas can be fun – and frustrating. The gymkhana competition is the poor relation of the average show – slotted into the schedule as an afterthought, often being completed as dusk descends and the rest of the showground is packing up. The competitions get the worst rosettes and the worst prizes, and only rarely is there a Victor Ludorum prize or the luxury and thrill of a trophy.

Yet, for most riders, the first experience of competitive riding is in mounted games, and gymkhanas provide an excellent introduction to the show ring. If your ambition is to be the best in the world at eventing, dressage or show jumping, there is every incentive to become the best at gymkhanas first.

Like any other activity, gymkhanas are more enjoyable if you perform well. And while it is indeed fun to take part, it is even more fun if you have a rosette to show for your pains. The aim of this book is to help you on your way.

While it is fun to take part, it is even more fun if you have a
rosette to show for your pains

# Chapter One

# THE GYMKHANA PONY

Riding is a partnership. In any form of competition, a good rider on a good horse has a reasonable chance of taking the honours, but however brilliant the rider a poor horse will not produce a winning performance, and a brilliant horse, without help from the rider, cannot reach the top alone.

This is often forgotten by the gymkhana competitor. Mounted games are meant to be fun, an enjoyable pastime in which the winning is less important than the taking part. This means that people frequently enter gymkhana events at the last minute, perhaps because they have been having a good time in other events in the show and are not ready to go home just yet.

Riders tend to rely on a willing pony, believing that he is the only means to a rosette. Indeed, failure is often blamed on the pony, as though the rider were an unimportant accessory. Losers – more often the parents of losers – have even been heard to suggest that members of games teams should not be allowed to enter

1

ordinary gymkhana events on the grounds that their presence is unfair to other competitors, forgetting that team members put in many hours of practice and that membership of a team squad is open to all.

Nevertheless, a good pony is clearly the starting point for a successful gymkhana career.

If you are looking for a suitable gymkhana pony, the following qualities are important. They can be roughly summarised under four headings:

1. Keenness
2. Conformation
3. Temperament
4. Intelligence

In addition, there are five other factors which will govern your personal choice:

5. Size
6. Age
7. Sex
8. Breeding
9. Price

Taking each of these headings in turn, there are not many ponies which would be awarded ten out of ten in every category. In judging a pony as a possible purchase, however, you should be able to assess at least his potential strengths and weaknesses.

## Keenness

A forward-going pony is essential. Many ponies do not enjoy mounted games. They display a reluctance to go

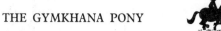

Many ponies display a reluctance to go up to the arena

up to the arena and, while not actually napping, are difficult to persuade into a canter. They reserve all their effort for the return journey, belting back home with enthusiasm and leaving their frustrated rider wishing they would display the same eagerness from the start. Their ears are rarely pricked and their whole demeanour is one of resignation. Their riders may describe them as lazy but this is not necessarily the case since in other circumstances – in work they really enjoy, such as going across country or jumping – they may be as keen and responsive as any rider could wish.

The *best* gymkhana pony shows obvious enjoyment of the games, tensing at the start, active and lively during a race.

## Conformation

Unless you are planning to use your pony for other competitive events, like working hunter or riding pony classes, the normal rules of conformation can be ignored. Such drawbacks as a goose rump, thin neck, large head or low withers can largely be disregarded. Check the length of the back – a long back may make sharp turns difficult for the pony to achieve – and look at him from the front. He should move straight and true. Avoid a pony with a narrow chest and girth. The nature of mounted games is activity in short bursts and therefore your pony should have room for his lungs to expand.

A high head carriage is an advantage as it helps the

rider in getting on and off at speed, but there is no need to reject a pony simply because he carries his head low. It merely means that you, as his rider, must adapt your riding technique to him.

If possible, ensure that he has a snaffle mouth. The Pony Club Prince Philip Cup competition will not allow any other bit to be used. Even if he requires a stronger bit for all other activities, in gymkhanas he will be expected to enter the ring in a snaffle.

What you are looking for above all is agility and suppleness. A pony that can cope with tight turns and can bend and weave with skill may make all the difference between winning and losing.

## Temperament

This covers the pony's outlook on life – his attitude to human beings and to other ponies. The latter is particularly important if you hope to take part in team events, but even in individual games you are not performing in isolation, as you would be, for example, in show jumping or eventing. A pony which lays back his ears and pulls faces at other ponies or, worse, kicks out at them is not a good gymkhana pony. It is particularly important that he should take crowding, even barging, in his stride.

As far as human beings are concerned, the more positive his approach the better. You and he are partners, and a good relationship needs to be built up as quickly as possible. A pony which trusts his rider

A pony which lays back his ears and pulls faces at other
ponies is not a good gymkhana pony

6

will accept all the curious demands that are made of him – bursting balloons, flags waving, sacks flapping round his legs – without getting into a panic.

He should be a pleasure to handle at all times: in the field (easy to catch), in the stable (easy to groom) and travelling (there is nothing more annoying than wondering whether your pony will load, or arriving late at a competition because it took you two hours to get him into the trailer: it is just as worrying if he is a restless traveller, sweating up and fretting, using up all the energy he should be saving for the games themselves). Of course he should also be reliable in traffic, unmoved by juggernauts, zippy sports cars, noisy motor cycles and ignorant drivers who toot their horns and overtake too close.

These virtues are not easy to assess when you try out a pony for the first time. The present owner is of course trying to put the pony in a good light, but very few sellers will deliberately lie to a prospective purchaser, even though they may conveniently forget to mention any drawbacks.

So, before you go to see the pony, prepare a list of questions to ask the owner. The questions should include:

1. How does he behave in traffic?
2. Are there any vehicles – lorries, tractors or motor cycles – which might cause problems?
3. Is he easy to catch?
4. Does he behave well in the stable and when being fed?

7

5. Has he ever, to your knowledge, had laminitis?
6. Does he suffer from sweet itch in the summer?
7. Will he load quietly and obediently?
8. Does he travel quietly?
9. Is he easy to shoe?
10. Is he nervous with vets?
11. Are his injections up to date?
12. Does he rear?
13. Does he buck?
14. Does he kick other ponies, or otherwise behave badly in company?
15. How does he react to men?

Some owners will allow you to have the pony on trial for anything up to a month, although this may depend on how anxious they are to make a sale. If they are reluctant to let you have him on trial, this does not necessarily mean that there is anything wrong with him. They may simply need to sell the pony quickly in order to buy another one.

It is usually considered a sensible precaution to have a pony vetted by an independent veterinary surgeon before buying, but if the purchase price of the pony is low (and many good gymkhana ponies do not cost much), the vet's charges may be more than you can afford. However, the vet will check the pony for soundness of lungs and limbs and will give you a rough idea of his age, but a very detailed examination, with blood tests and X-rays, will cost a great deal of money. If you do decide to get a vet's report, make certain that he knows what you are buying the pony for and where and how you plan to keep the pony.

## Intelligence

In ponies intelligence is measured by how long they take to learn. Constant repetition is usually recommended as the best method for getting a horse to understand what is expected of him, and this is as true of gymkhana ponies as of any other horse.

The problem with repetition is that it can lead to boredom, and boredom leads to stubbornness. Who hasn't heard of the good jumper which has suddenly decided not to jump any more? Fortunately, mounted games, even in practice, offer sufficient variety and excitement to keep a pony interested and excited. A good games pony rarely gets bored with gymkhana events: an intelligent one learns to anticipate, even to the extent of watching the starter's flag or manoeuvring himself into the best position for his rider to carry out the tasks required.

Intelligence, however, is not easy to assess when viewing a pony for the first time. The best you can do is to see how much interest the pony shows in everything that is going on around him. If he seems bright and alert, the chances are that he is clever and adaptable, a quick learner and, potentially, a good buy.

The remaining five factors are governed by personal preference or restrictions.

## Size

Pony Club Prince Philip Cup rules place an upper limit on the size of a games pony at 14.2 hh, with a half-inch allowance for shoes. In an ordinary gymkhana, such a rule rarely exists, but most horses over this height are at a disadvantage anyway, finding tight turns difficult to make and being too tall for rapid remounting. There is no minimum height limit in any competition but, in the Pony Club, riders weighing more than 8 stones 5 pounds, dressed for competing, may not ride a pony 12.2 hh and under. Here again, this is not a rule usually found at ordinary gymkhanas, but a rider who is clearly too big or too heavy for a very small pony could be asked to withdraw.

The size of a gymkhana pony, therefore, depends on your own size and weight. In addition, your own age can determine the pony you are looking for. If you are a Pony Club member, hoping to take part in all kinds of competition – not only mounted games – you will be looking for a good all-rounder. Most Prince Philip Cup teams are made up of ponies which will carry their riders round a novice cross-country course one day, tackle a show-jumping course the next and play a major part in a Prince Philip competition the following week. They will be capable of attending rallies – indeed, *all* Prince Philip ponies must attend a certain number of working rallies during the year – as well as coping with the demands of Pony Club camp.

Generally speaking, therefore, the best games ponies are between 12.2 and 13.2 hh.

The difference between a small pony and a large one is usually the difference between agility and speed. Small ponies have the advantage in races involving twisting and turning; larger ponies are faster but can waste time in a race such as bending by taking too wide a turn around the end pole. From the rider's point of view, jumping on at speed is easier on a small pony but jumping off a bigger pony is safer and often faster than the same action from a little one. The reason for this is the extra length of neck in front of the rider and the extra amount of pony available for you to place a steadying hand against.

## Age

Almost all games competitions at whatever level have an embargo on the use of ponies under four years of age. A three-year-old in pony terms is still a baby even though he may be broken to the saddle and going well under a rider. The principal reason for this is that gymkhanas put too great a strain on immature muscles and tendons. In fact, young ponies in general – that is, up to the age of seven or eight – should be taken very gently through their games training and never asked to compete at too high a level. The prime age is between nine and eighteen, although good, experienced ponies are capable of continuing well into their twenties and have even been known to change hands for a four figure sum long after their twentieth birthday.

If, however, you are buying a games pony for the first time, the best age to choose is eleven or twelve.

11

## Sex

Some people will only ride mares; others stick to geldings. The lovers of mares will swear that they are more intelligent, more responsive, more affectionate. Devotees of geldings apply the same virtues but add reliability. The truth is that ponies are individuals just as much as people and one mare can be as different from another as a gelding can.

By and large it is better to segregate the sexes so that, if you are lucky enough to have a lot of horses and ponies and plenty of grazing, you keep geldings in one field and mares in another. That way there is less likelihood of jealousies and rivalries building up.

Some mares can be particularly 'mare-ish', behaving quite skittishly when they are in season, developing inconvenient attachments to other horses and displaying a total lack of attention whenever the object of their affection is around. This can be a severe drawback if you are taking part in a competition at the time.

In the end, the decision about the sex of your pony may well depend on where you keep it. If you share a field with other pony-owners, consult them first. It could save a great deal of distress and avoid a situation in which you are forced to make alternative arrangements at the last minute, simply because the gelding-owners in your field are not prepared to welcome with open arms the wonderful little mare you have just bought.

## Breeding

This is a fairly minor consideration if a good games pony is all that you are looking for. A large number of excellent ponies are of indeterminate breed and certainly not distinguished by entry in anybody's stud book. Small ponies tend to be predominantly Welsh, bigger ones New Forest, but a long pedigree is really not important. It only becomes a prominent factor in your choice if you plan to use the pony for showing classes. This is not as far-fetched as it sounds; many excellent Prince Philip team ponies are winners in other fields, particularly working hunter pony classes or show ponies of hunter type.

## Price

First-class games ponies can be expensive, especially if their owners can advertise them as having reached Wembley (Prince Philip Cup final) or the county championship (Mounted Games Association of Great Britain). But games ponies can also be gratifyingly cheap, especially if they are small and fast and you yourself are lightweight, athletic and a confident rider. If price is a limiting factor in your search for a gymkhana pony, then look for a pony which is too fizzy for beginners and too 'ordinary' for the show ring but has many of the qualities described earlier in this chapter. With careful training you can soon turn your ugly duckling into a swan.

# Chapter Two

# TRAINING TIPS FOR PONY AND RIDER

There are two schools of thought with regard to gymkhana ponies. Some trainers believe that it is better to buy a proven games pony, one that has behind it an established record of competition at a high level; others prefer to start from scratch with one that is totally new to games.

Certainly an experienced pony is an important factor in a successful partnership. The danger is that, while the rider is learning technique, the pony gradually slips into bad habits, and the rider, unable to match the pony's ability, becomes disheartened. When both are learning together, improvement is gradual but positive.

There is no doubt that the best way to learn how to win at gymkhanas is to join a team-training squad. If you are under fifteen years of age, you should first take out a subscription to the Pony Club and then join the Prince Philip squad of your branch. Fortunately, there are very few branches which do not take part in mounted games; if you have the bad luck to live in an area where interest in games is non-existent, speak to your District Commissioner who may be able to arrange for you to transfer to a neighbouring branch.

Alternatively, it could be possible for you to drum up enthusiasm among your friends, find an adult to help you with your training and form a squad yourself. If this solution is not feasible, enquire from the Mounted Games Association of Great Britain whether your county runs a team and contact the county trainer direct. In the latter situation, however, remember that the MGAGB is open to riders up to twenty-one years old and, while training will be given to you freely, willingly and indeed enthusiastically, you will be up against some very experienced riders and ponies when it comes to team selection.

Remember, too, that whatever squad you join all team training requires members to attend practices regularly. You will have to be ready to travel to practices, and for this you may require transport and a willing driver (parent or friend) to give up spare time to take you to a practice, wait around while the practice is going on and bring you home again at the end, and not just occasionally but once or twice a week. However, very often the long-suffering driver, who starts off as an observer, ends up as a willing worker, putting up equipment, helping with training and acting as a line steward at competitions. By the time this stage has been reached, your enthusiasm will have spread and mounted games will have become a family affair.

Although you and your pony do your training together, there are in fact two aspects to the training programme. Your pony must learn to start, stop, neck-rein and turn, while you learn vaulting, dismounting, and general dexterity and agility.

Practising is not just running through the various games: different games need different skills. However, once you have mastered the basic skills required you merely have to learn the rules for each new game.

Inevitably, the process of bringing your pony to a high standard of obedience takes a long time. Try not to get too impatient with him, and remember that practising can be carried out at any time. Most important of all, do not practise for too long. Ten minutes of successful training is worth far more than half an hour of struggle.

Begin by deciding exactly what you must teach your pony.

## PONY TRAINING

### Starting

This is one of the earliest lessons learned by a pony – moving forward from a stationary position to a walk. If he has been properly broken in and his schooling has continued quietly and sensibly throughout his life, he will respond rapidly to the aids, the pressure of your legs on his sides and the relaxation of your fingers on the reins: sometimes reinforced by a spoken command, they mean 'Go forward'. Each transition from pace to pace has its own code of signals which you will have been taught at riding school lessons and which you will practise at Pony Club rallies. Almost certainly, your instructor will have told you to make the transitions both up and down the paces in an orderly and gradual manner.

In mounted games, however, the last thing you want is a slow progression through the paces. If that is what you get from your pony, you will barely be into a canter by the time your opponents have crossed the finishing line. The poor old games pony has to learn a whole new set of rules. Pressure on his sides now means leapfrogging the normal changes of pace and going straight from a standstill into a full-blown gallop. It means forgetting the niceties of schooling and getting from one point to another as quickly as possible as soon as his rider gives the signal. At the same time, if he is to be an all-round Pony Club pony, he must not be allowed to forget his normal manners because, by the very nature of Pony Club activities, he could be competing in a mounted games contest one week and tackling a dressage test the next.

Fortunately, ponies are versatile creatures and can learn to behave in the way that is expected of them. Association is an important factor in learning ability – see how quickly a pony comes to connect the rattle of a bucket with food or a hand in your pocket with a titbit. Similarly, the sight and sound of games equipment will help to teach your pony the right sort of behaviour for the occasion. Reinforce this by never practising on your own without getting out suitable equipment. You need only a few items – a cone with a flag in it, two or three bending poles, some pieces of litter and a cane. If possible, enlist the help of a friend.

In any race, a good start is essential. Your pony should be able to stand behind the start line, tensed up and ready to spring into a gallop the moment the starter drops his flag. So ask a friend to take the role of the starter, positioning her a few yards in front and to the side of an imaginary start line. Give her a 4-foot cane with a triangular pennant attached and invite her to lower it when she thinks you are ready to start. Try to vary the lapse of time between the moment you are in position and the dropping of the flag. In an actual race there will be up to six ponies waiting for the starting signal and it only takes one to misbehave to delay or upset the others.

Concentrate on getting your pony to stand *still*. It is important for a quick getaway for you to have complete confidence in your pony's good behaviour. That way, you can keep your eye – and your mind – on the starter. If all your attention is taken up with controlling the pony, you could miss the moment the starter's flag drops, and in good quality company a stride or two missed at the start is very difficult to make up during the race.

There are some unscrupulous trainers who in the past

Your pony should be tensed up and ready to spring into a
gallop the moment the starter drops his flag

have actively encouraged ponies to misbehave on the start line. It is believed – with some justification – that a troublesome pony, one for example which is turning round or plunging forward, draws the starter's eye so that he or she watches the difficult pony and, concerned about undue delay, lowers the flag at the exact moment the troublemaker is facing the right way. This should never be part of your tactics on how to win at gymkhanas. Fortunately, most experienced starters now recognise the gambit and will order recalcitrant ponies to be held some six yards behind the rest.

## Stopping

This is another action for which a pony has to unlearn the lessons given in normal schooling. The gradual descent through the paces has no place in gymkhana games. Most games require ponies to gallop flat out in short bursts, coming to a shuddering halt at the point where the rider has an action to carry out. This means instant obedience to the rider's aids – the squeeze of the legs and the tightening of the hand on the rein.

The rider's voice is a vital aid in this aspect of training – something which is often forgotten by young riders. Perhaps they feel foolish talking to their ponies or maybe they just forget. But a pony is very responsive to the human voice and will recognise the tone even if the actual words are nonsense.

So make good use of your voice, particularly in the early stages of training. When you want your pony to

There are all manner of games where a pony standing like a
rock will save valuable seconds

stop, apply the stop aids and accompany them with a firm 'Whoa!' or 'Stop!' The actual word is unimportant, but it is best to use the same one each time. If you want your pony to slow down, use the stopping aids less forcefully and say something like 'Gently!', drawing the word out slowly and quietly.

To begin with, your pony is likely to stop when told but will move off again as soon as you relax your hold. Concentrate on getting him to stand still until given the signal to proceed. There are all manner of games where a pony standing like a rock will save valuable seconds when his rider is trying, for example, to insert a flag into a cone or stand a bottle on a table.

## Neck-reining

This means teaching your pony to respond to the pressure of the reins on his neck, so that when he feels the right rein on his neck he moves to the left, and vice versa. It is an important part of Western riding technique developed to enable a cowboy to use only one hand in controlling his horse while swinging a lariat or leading a pack horse with the other. One-handed control is just as important in mounted games where most races require the rider to carry a piece of equipment.

To start with, you will have to exaggerate the action by using both hands on the rein. You should hold your hands higher than usual and move them in the direction you wish to go. For example, assuming you wish to go to the left, take your hands firmly to the left, putting clear pressure on the left side of the bit and resting the right rein against the neck and crest. Use the leg aids to control the pony's quarters.

Gradually reduce the pressure on the bit and concentrate on the neck rein. Soon you will find that only a very slight movement of the hand is needed to ensure a response. Indeed, it is the *slight* movement that makes neck-reining effective because anything sharp and jerky will give the opposite signal to your pony. The hand on the reins should be held palm downwards and the wrist must be kept supple and slightly flexed. To indicate a wish to change direction, apply the leg aids *first* and then make a very small turn of the wrist towards the direction you want to go.

**Turning**

The ability to turn sharply is a vital ingredient in acquiring gymkhana skills. Most ponies which take part in gymkhanas only occasionally (however willing they may be), tend to take a wide turn around the end bending pole (for example), thus reducing any advantage they may have gained by rapid progress through the poles. Some ponies, because of their conformation, will never be supple enough to carry out a very tight turn, but the rider should nevertheless know how to position them for the turn in order to reduce the disadvantage to a minimum.

Positioning is therefore extremely important. At the start of a race, the pony is facing straight up the line of equipment. At the turn, the rider should manoeuvre so that the pony is facing straight back down the line before the return journey begins.

With a tight turn at the top, this position is usually achieved. But it is still possible to minimise the disadvantage of a wide turn, if that is all you can do, by following the correct line. If for example your line up the row of bending poles means that you will be passing to the left side of the last pole and making a right-handed turn, you should guide your pony well to the left of the pole and make your turn so that you re-enter the row of poles straight. So many inexperienced

The best line to take through bending poles. If necessary take a wide turn round the end in order to re-enter the poles straight

riders underestimate the size of the turning circle and re-enter the poles at an angle. It will be several strides before they are back on the right course, by which time the race is lost. The illustration on p.24 shows the line you should take, and this applies to all races where the top turn has to be carried out at speed.

A pony that starts, stops and stands on command, neck-reins and turns in his own length, and is very fast in between these manoeuvres, is a priceless games pony which will quickly earn a well-deserved reputation. With a rider capable of matching his abilities, the combination is almost unbeatable. And this is where rider training comes in.

## RIDER TRAINING

### Vaulting

Mounting in the conventional way is time wasting. By the time you have gathered up your reins, put your foot in the stirrup, grasped the cantle and swung yourself up into the saddle, your opponents are on their way back to the finishing line. If your pony is not as good at standing still as you would like him to be, you could well be hopping around for what will seem like hours before you finally get back on your pony and continue the race. It is essential to learn the vault.

You need to be exceptionally athletic before you can vault
easily on to a *stationary* pony

The most important thing to remember about the vault is that it is the forward momentum of the pony which carries the rider into the saddle. You need to be exceptionally athletic or to have a very small pony before you can vault easily on to a stationary pony.

The vault can be broken down into stages:

**a.** The pony should be travelling straight at a steady trot.

**b.** The rider runs alongside the pony's shoulder, facing forwards but with the upper part of the body twisted so that the left hand, holding the reins, rests on the pony's crest and the right arm is across the pommel with the right hand grasping the front of the saddle flap.

**c.** The rider watches the pony's stride, waiting for the nearside forefoot to hit the ground.

**d.** At this point, the rider jumps with both feet together and as the spring carries her upwards swings her right leg across the saddle, taking her weight on her right arm and shoulder.

These stages are, of course, completed at speed so that the vault appears to be carried out in one fluid movement. Timing and control are vital. Timing picks the right moment for your upward spring; control prevents your leap from taking you right over the pony and off the other side.

Control is also important to ensure that once in the saddle you can stop the pony or slow him down before you have to meet the next challenge – putting a ball into

The Vault

Grasp the saddle with your right hand, the crest with your left

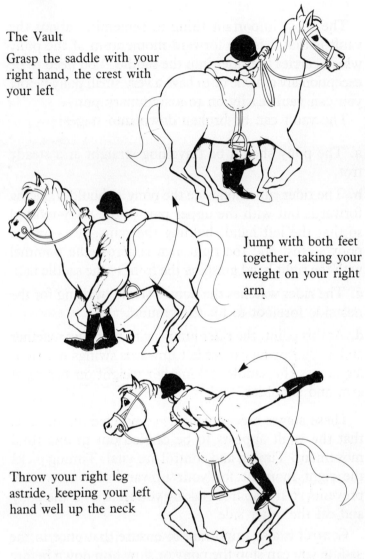

Jump with both feet together, taking your weight on your right arm

Throw your right leg astride, keeping your left hand well up the neck

a bucket or handing over equipment to the next member of the team.

The vault is not easy to describe and, to begin with, even less easy to carry out. But, like riding a bicycle, once learned the technique is never forgotten. It can be practised at any time – out hacking, bringing your pony from the field, at a formal training session. If possible, train yourself to vault from both sides; there are plenty of occasions in mounted games when the ability to get on from the 'off' side can make the difference between winning and losing a race.

## Dismounting

Reins in the left hand, which rests just in front of the withers, right hand on the pommel, feet out of stirrups, right leg swinging across the saddle, land lightly at the pony's shoulder, facing forwards. A routine manoeuvre which every beginner learns at the first lesson.

Dismounting in gymkhanas is in essence no different; it is simply carried out more swiftly and with no slackening of the pony's speed. The important 'extra' is that as soon as your feet touch the ground you should start running. If necessary, use your right hand on your pony's neck to steady yourself. *But do not stand still.* If you do, you will end up flat on your face on the ground.

As with vaulting, practise dismounting on both sides and at any time when you and your pony are out together.

In both manoeuvres, vaulting and dismounting, a pony with a high head carriage is an advantage because you can use his neck to support and steady you. A pony with a low head carriage or a small pony with not much in front will require you to take special care.

## Dexterity

This is the particular quality which will enable you to carry out the requirements of different races. You have to develop co-ordination between hand and eye, so that flags do not miss holes in cones, and bottles are placed accurately on upturned bins. Some people are naturally dexterous, but even clumsy riders can learn to improve their skills with practice.

The more opportunity you have to handle equipment the better. There is no right or wrong way, as such, to hold an item and you will in due course find the method that suits you best, but if you are new to gymkhanas the following guidelines might help you.

**Flags** The easiest way to insert a flag into a cone is to hold it like a sword. If the rules of the race call for you to start with a flag then there is no problem involved in holding it in the most advantageous way as soon as it is handed to you at the beginning of the race. When, however, you have to collect a flag from one cone and insert it into another, the easiest and most natural means of grasping it while it is still in the cone is to take it with the palm facing forwards, thumb uppermost. Now,

Hold the flag like a sword when inserting it into a cone

Pick up a flag with your palm facing forward, always taking the one furthest from you

you are holding it like a lance. Before you deposit it, therefore, you will have to change your grip and, if possible, change it before you reach the other cone. So before you take part in a flag race, practise adjusting your hold on the flag until you are able to alter it without slackening speed or dropping the flag.

**Mugs** There are two types of mugs commonly used in gymkhana games. One is beaker-shaped, usually made of plastic. The other is a metal mug, broad-based with straight sides and a handle.

The beaker is used where mugs have to be stacked one on top of the other, generally on a bending pole. It is easy to handle and, because it is taken from the top of one pole for transfer to another, it is held in the same way for both manoeuvres. Four or five beakers in a stack are surprisingly stable provided you do not use too much force when adding a new mug to the stack. If you try to jam it in place you run the risk of making the stack bounce – and fall off. Quietness and steadiness are therefore the key factors in handling beakers.

Metal mugs are harder to manipulate, particularly if your hands are small. They may be used in races where a mug has to be transferred from one pole to another or from an upturned bin to a pole. In the former case, it is possible to grasp the mug by the handle and to manoeuvre it without altering your grip. But in the second example, it is best to ignore the handle. The mug, inverted on a bin or table, will be roughly level with your feet when you are mounted so that it is natural

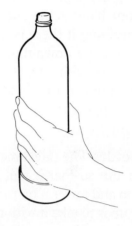

a. Pick up a mug from above

a. Pick up a bottle with your hand facing forward

b. Transfer your grip to the handle if necessary

b. Transfer your grip ready for the drop

to grasp it from above when you are picking it up. If your hand is big enough and you are confident of not dropping it there is no need to change your grip when carrying it down the arena and depositing it on the pole. Anyone with a small hand, however, may have to switch the hold to the handle. The easiest way to do this is to support the mug against your chest while you shift your hand.

**Bottles** The safest method of placing a bottle on a table or bin so that it will not fall over is to hold it by the top and lower it on to the stand. The easiest way to pick it up is to take it with the hand facing forwards, grasping it round the body of the bottle. Now, unless you change your grip you will run the risk of knocking it over as you put it back on the table. So practise shifting your hand to the top of the bottle while you are on the move, steadying the bottle by resting the base on the pommel of your saddle.

**Balls** Most races using tennis balls as part of the equipment are precision events. The ball must be plucked from the top of a cone and placed on the top of another. Always approach the cone at an oblique angle and turn your hand so that the palm faces backwards. That way, if you fumble the pick-up, the ball is more likely to fall into your hand. When placing the ball on to the cone, grip it by the fingertips to make the manoeuvre more accurate.

When placing a ball into a bucket, *never* throw it, not even as a desperate measure. If you should overshoot

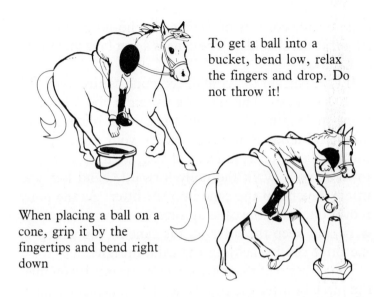

To get a ball into a bucket, bend low, relax the fingers and drop. Do not throw it!

When placing a ball on a cone, grip it by the fingertips and bend right down

the bucket, you will find that less time is wasted by pulling up and returning. Even if a throw were accurate, there would be a real risk of the force of the throw causing the ball to bounce out of the bucket. The answer is to bend as low to the bucket as you can and relax your fingers so that the ball just rolls into the container.

Rolled-up socks are sometimes used in place of tennis balls. In principle, you should handle them in the same way, but many riders choose to place the sock between their teeth when vaulting on and galloping back up the arena.

**Litter** Picking up litter with a cane requires considerable dexterity and practice. The litter usually provided for these events consists of washing-up liquid containers, cut off at the shoulder. The cane is 4 feet long and made of bamboo.

It is important to maintain as much control over the cane as you can. This means grasping it about halfway along its length. If you hold the cane at one end, the other end tends to waver. Position your pony so that the piece of litter is in front of you, with its open end towards you. Walk the pony forward, bend low and insert the end of the cane into the litter. As the pony moves on, bring the cane up sharply with a twist of the wrist and keep the litter on the cane as you gallop to the litter bin by holding the cane upright.

The position of the pony is all important. If you miss the piece of litter the first time or it falls off the cane, take the pony back and try again. Never waste time

To collect litter, manoeuvre so that the open end is towards you, then bend down to get the cane as low as possible

trying to flick the litter round until its open end is towards you. Your pony is mobile and manoeuvrable, a washing-up liquid container is not.

**Rings** If you have to hang rings on to a hook, turn your pony sideways on so that your field of action is wide. Avoid taking the pony in head-on. Not only will the pony tend to back away, but leaning forward and stretching over his ears will put you both off balance and give you no leeway at all for mistakes.

**Egg and spoon** or **ball and racquet** In both these events a round rollable object has to be kept in place without being touched by hand. Use the forward momentum of the pony to control the equipment by tipping the

Tipping the racquet slightly downwards helps keep the ball on

end of the racquet or spoon slightly downwards. If you hold it straight or tipped upwards, the ball will roll out towards you.

## Agility

To a certain extent, agility can be acquired; provided, of course, that you are prepared to work at it. If you are really keen, join a gymnastics club, where learning the exercises that will make your body supple and strong is more fun than trying to carry out a fitness routine on your own.

Saving time is all important in successful gymkhana riding. Most riders, however experienced, make mistakes occasionally. If you can correct your errors rapidly, you will be able to beat the accurate but slow performer, so practise picking up fallen equipment without dismounting. This can be quite difficult unless you are really agile and quick, but if you can grab a fallen flag or dropped ball without slackening speed or falling off, you are arming yourself with yet another skill, all part of how to win at gymkhanas.

# Chapter Three

# GYMKHANA EVENTS

There are more than fifty different gymkhana events in popular use but most of them fall into three different categories: those that depend on speed, those that call for precision and those that are a combination of the two. There is one further category: luck. A few games rely entirely on luck to produce a winner. However good you are and however hard you practise, there is no way in which you can ensure success in this category.

But the others are a different matter. This chapter analyses the various races most usually found in gymkhana schedules, looks at the qualities a competitor needs to be in the ribbons and gives tips on how to achieve them.

## SPEED EVENTS

### Bending

The first and by far the most popular event – almost all gymkhana schedules contain a bending race. Unless

39

the organiser is unable to get hold of bending poles, this will head the list in all age groups. It is purely a speed event and precision hardly enters into it, so, excluding some form of disaster, a fast pony will always beat a slow one.

Where two fast ponies compete against each other, the winner will be the one which takes the shortest line. This means hugging the poles as you weave between them and taking as tight a turn as possible round the last pole. To encourage your pony to bend economically, use the weight of your body to guide him

Bending technique
a. Bending your body with the pony helps to guide him through the poles

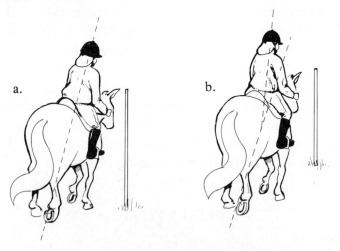

b. If the line of your body does not follow the pony's, you will unbalance him and slow down your progress by leaning towards the pole you are passing. Keep your inside leg on the girth and your outside one just behind the girth to control his hindquarters. Your knees should hug the saddle to avoid striking the poles as you go. Hitting a pole with your knee is not only painful but, worse, could break or dislodge the pole and possibly (if the pole ends up flat on the ground) disqualify you.

## Apple Bobbing

If you hate getting your head wet, you will never do well at apple bobbing. Wherever the bucket of water containing the apple is placed in the race, your object is to get there as quickly as possible, leap off your pony and dive into the bucket so that you can anchor the apple on the bottom and sink your teeth into it. Then you replace your hat, do up the chinstrap, vault back on and gallop home. Do not be tempted to continue the race without replacing your hat and *fastening* the chinstrap – winning is never more important than safety. Practise mounting and dismounting and doing up the chinstrap, three areas where time can be saved.

## Dressing-up

If your pony will stand still on a loose rein while you don the various items of clothing provided by the organisers (usually shirts, pyjama jackets, hats and scarves), your hands will be free to do up buttons, etc. Concentrate on training your pony to stand still on command.

HOW TO WIN AT GYMKHANAS

... leap off your pony and dive into the bucket

## Gretna Green

This race requires you to gallop to the far end of the arena, pick up a passenger pillion-style, and gallop to the finish. Time can be saved if your partner can mount quickly. Leapfrogging over your pony's tail is possibly the quickest method of getting on but you must be absolutely confident that your pony will accept such an unorthodox means of mounting. Otherwise, your partner should be able to throw her leg over the pony's quarters and sit astride behind you in one easy movement. You and your friend should practise mounting technique.

## Groom's Stakes

This event is popular in team competitions – that is, it is popular with organisers if not with competitors. The game involves leading a riderless pony between bending poles and picking up the rider at the other end. Practise leading a pony by his rein so that both ponies can canter – even gallop – in perfect harmony. Remember, when weaving between poles, to leave sufficient room for both ponies to pass a pole without knocking it over (see illustration on p.44).

## Jelly Baby Gobble

This race is similar to apple bobbing. The rider has to grab a jelly baby from a plate of flour with her teeth, remount and ride to the finish. You cannot be fastidious

The line of each pony in the Groom's
Stakes. Alternatively, the waiting rider
can stand with her back to the incoming
ponies and turn after the changeover

In the Rope Race, one rider peels off
at the end while the other turns
sharply and picks up the third
member of the team

44

about getting flour on your face, and you must be able to dismount and remount quickly.

## Lead and Run

Teach your pony to lead willingly. Then it is up to you to run as fast as you can to the far end, vault on and gallop to the finish. Your pony should canter beside you while you are running. Practise leading your pony by the rein without pulling him in the mouth. The reverse of this race, **Run and Lead,** is sometimes better for ponies which do not lead well, provided you can get off without stopping the pony. He may not realise that he is being led until you are nearly home.

## Musical Mats

This is another race which requires a willing leader. You must dismount *as soon as you hear the music stop* and before turning into the centre; then lead your pony to a vacant mat. While the music is playing and you are riding round the perimeter of the circle, position yourself so that there is plenty of space between you and the riders in front and behind. The chances are that you will find a vacant mat close by and undisputed. If you cannot avoid bunching, a common problem early on in the race, note the competitors who have difficulty getting off or whose pony leads reluctantly and stay close to them. If it comes to a race for a mat, you will have the edge.

45

Sometimes the perimeter of the circle is marked by jump stands: always speed up as you pass a stand to avoid getting caught behind it when the music stops.

## Musical Wands

Except for dismounting, which is not required in this race, follow the advice given for musical mats.

## Postman's Chase

Bending is usually a part of this event, so practise the technique described for bending. In addition, you have to place a 'letter' in a sack, which you may do on your return journey. Use the weight of your body to guide the pony between the poles while you concentrate on inserting the letter into the sack.

## Rope Race

In this partnership event, where two riders, holding the opposite ends of a short piece of rope, have to bend up and down a line of poles, it is important that the two ponies move well and willingly together (see the illustration on p.44). The race will be lost if one pony hangs back. With a friend, practise manoeuvring as a pair and make certain as you pass between the poles that you leave enough room for both ponies. Remember also that one of you will have to neck-rein with the right hand. It is very important in all games techniques to become equally proficient with right and left hands and to be able to get on and off with speed and dexterity from either side.

## Sack Race

Sack races are won or lost by how quickly you can get into the sack. Movement in the sack is, of course, also important, but most people develop their own technique and are not happy with any other. The shufflers stick their toes into the corners of the sack and run for the finish with short, rapid steps. Jumpers, on the other hand, move forward in a series of small leaps. Both methods are effective, but jumping is more tiring and shuffling is difficult if the grass is long. Practise whichever method you prefer, but concentrate on picking up a sack from the ground and getting into it. Most sack race rules state that you cannot put your feet into the sack *before* you dismount, so there is no point in trying this system.

## Saddling Up

In a race where you have to ride bareback to your saddle, put it on and ride to the finish, speed and deftness in doing up buckles is vital. Concentrate on positioning the saddle correctly but do not waste time in pulling your pony's leg forwards to reduce wrinkling under the girth. Unless the rules state that the feet have to be in the stirrups before you cross the finishing line, do not bother to pull the stirrup irons down. In an **Unsaddling Race,** practise running up the stirrups – if necessary before you have dismounted. Never be tempted to fling the saddle down – there is no point in damaging the saddle for the sake of winning a race. Unless a horizontal pole is provided to rest the saddle on place it carefully on the ground with the weight taken on the pommel.

## Canter; Trot and Walk; Trotting; Walk, Trot and Canter

These are all races where the rider is penalised for breaking into a faster pace by having to circle her pony before continuing. Concentrate on training your pony to stride out on a free rein without being tempted to break. These races are not very popular with competitors because they are boring, but gymkhana organisers love them because they need no equipment. They are, however, very difficult to judge, and if you choose to enter them you must be prepared for your nearest rival to get away without penalty for cantering when she should be trotting or trotting when she should be walking. If this should happen, however hard done by you may feel, there is no point in complaining. The race will not be run again.

## Tyre Race

This is a popular team race, sometimes held for individuals. It calls for a rider to dismount, climb through a lightweight motor-cycle tyre, remount and ride to the finish. In a team race, your pony will be held by a fellow team member while you negotiate the tyre. In an individual race, your pony has to be held by you.

Opinions differ as to whether it is quicker to lift the tyre, put it over your head, and allow it to drop down your body, or to jump into the tyre, feet first, and then raise it up your body and over your head in one swift movement. On the whole, the first method is the one favoured by experienced competitors, but you should try both methods out at home and practise the one which suits you best. If you have to hold your pony yourself while negotiating the tyre, the manoeuvre is bound to be awkward but concentrate on practising your technique. Dismounting and vaulting should also be practised.

## VC Race

The object of this race is to collect a sack loosely filled with straw and carry it back to the finish (an action representing the heroic rescue of a comrade from the field of battle – hence the Victoria Cross Race). You can carry it any way you like – in one hand or across the pommel of your saddle. If you choose the latter, beware of VC races where bending is involved. A straw-filled sack sticks out quite a long way on either side of your pony and you must be careful that it does not knock against the bending poles as you pass.

# PRECISION EVENTS

Although the aim of these races is to finish ahead of your rivals, the emphasis here is on care and consistency. Speed can lead to mistakes, and mistakes can lose you the race. Practise until you are confident that you can complete the allotted task accurately every time. Then, even if your pony is a little on the slow side, you have a good chance of success.

## Aunt Sally

Included in this category are all those races which require you to throw a ball or small bean bag into, onto, or at another item of equipment. It is important that your pony should stand still so that your attention is not distracted and your throwing arm is not jogged. Practise at home, throwing tennis balls at tin cans or bean bags into a bucket. Time yourself, and see how often your throw is successful.

## Ball and Cone

The object of this game is to balance a tennis ball on the top of a cone or to transfer a ball from one cone to another. Placing the ball on to the cone cannot be carried out at speed, and even though you may approach the cone at a gallop you will have to check your pony before bending down towards the cone. Try to angle your approach. This has the effect of slowing the pony down and allows you, if necessary, to circle the cone as you grasp the ball or put it in place. There is no substitute in this instance for having your own cone and tennis ball to practise with.

## Egg and Spoon

Rules for this race vary. You may be asked to ride to an egg and spoon on the ground, dismount and carry the egg in the spoon to the finish, leading your pony with the other hand. The egg may be in the spoon to begin with or you could have to scoop it up off the ground. Some organisers hand you the egg and spoon at the start and ask you to carry it up and down a row of bending poles. In all cases you are not allowed to touch the egg with your hand.

This is a race where steadiness is more important than speed. It can easily be practised at home, but remember to hardboil the egg first!

## Musical Statues

Teach your pony to stand stock still on command and your chances will be good in this event. It is probably not possible to train him not to flick an ear or swish his tail (musical statues can be lost on these movements), but he can learn to come to a four-square halt when the music stops and not to take even one step forward until you give him the signal (see the section on 'Stopping' in Chapter Two).

## Pyramid Race

Because of the care needed in building up the pyramid, this event falls into the precision category. Though there may be local variations, the rules require you to transfer four or five 1-litre ice cream containers, weighted with sand and sealed, from one table to another. Usually the containers are placed side by side on the first table but have to be piled one on top of the other on the second. In both cases, their position is not very stable and it is just as easy to knock one container off the table when picking up its neighbour as it is to build a leaning tower of containers which will tumble as soon as the final one is put in place.

Speed between the tables is valuable but not as important as a steady pony which will stand obediently

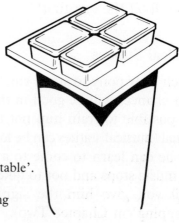

Ice cream containers on a 'table'. Take the container furthest from you to avoid disturbing the others

as you deposit the container on the second table. Practise circling the first table, collecting the container while on the move. Always take the one furthest from you so that if you fumble the pick-up you are less likely to knock any of the others down. You will have to pull your pony up completely when depositing the container, especially as the 'pyramid' gets taller.

## Water Race

This is another 'transferring' race where steadiness of hand and movement will usually beat the mad dash. A pony with a smooth, regular canter is a great asset, particularly if he is obedient and stands still. Water has to be carried in a beaker or mug from a bucket at one end of the arena to a large jug or vase at the other, each competitor trying to transfer as much as she can in a given time. The ability to control the pony one-handed is vital as it is impossible to hold the mug and the reins in the same hand without spilling the water. Practise carrying water at home on your own pony, building up as much speed as you can.

## COMBINED SPEED AND PRECISION EVENTS

Some of the best-loved gymkhana games fall into this category, and many of them make up the programme for a team competition. Practice and yet more practice is the only way to get better than anyone else, and even then it is all too easy to make a fatal mistake.

## Ball and Bucket

This game and related races, such as the **Potato Race** and the **Old Sock Race,** provide a combination of almost all the skills you have learned. You must dismount to collect the ball, potato or old sock, remount before placing the item in a bucket and ride as fast as you can between the items of equipment. Most experienced riders get off their ponies well before they reach the pile of tennis balls, leading the pony the last few yards. It is one of the few games where the pony does not have to reach the far line and even the rider on foot does not have to cross it.

Team competitions have a different method of playing Ball and Bucket, in that each rider starts with a ball, puts it in the bucket on the way up the arena, collects another ball and rides back to give it to the next member of the team. Only the last to go has to put the ball in the bucket on the way back. Individual competitions ask each rider to transfer a number of balls one at a time from a pile at the far end to the bucket in the centre of her lane. The two competitions, in effect, test different skills.

The individual rider can make fast progress on her initial run, but then her vault has to be absolutely foolproof if she is to be back on her pony before the bucket is reached. She then has to turn on her tracks to collect another ball. She loses out on the time and space available for her vault but gains in the putting of the ball into the bucket. It is much easier to be accurate in this operation if you are circling the bucket. It is only on her final run that she has to bend really low to the bucket in order to get the ball in without slackening speed.

The team rider needs to be travelling at top speed as she passes the bucket and to time the dropping of the ball so that it neither bounces out nor causes her to check her rate of progress. She has more time for her vault, however, unless she is the last rider in the team, as she does not have to be astride her pony until she is close to the finishing line.

The keen games player is probably both a team and an individual rider. Mastery of all the skills, therefore, is essential, and you should practise placing objects in a bucket, bending as low as possible. Ideally, your hand should be below the rim of the bucket before you release the ball. You should also practise your vault.

## Ball and Racquet

The ability to control your pony with one hand is particularly important in this race in which you have to carry a ball balanced on a tennis racquet up and down a row of bending poles. Your attention will be focused on keeping the ball in place and it will be easier to build up speed if your pony responds to neck-reining. Practising, therefore, should concentrate on this aspect, as well as on the actual carrying of a ball on a racquet. You will find it easier if you tip the head of the racquet forwards slightly.

## Balloon Bursting

Bursting balloons by means of a cane with a pin taped to the end crops up whenever a gymkhana organiser is prepared to spend some time blowing the balloons up. Variations exist in the method of anchoring the balloons as some organisers will peg them to a sack or board on the ground while others tie them to a framework at head height. The ground method is the most usual. First of all practise bursting balloons dismounted which will tell you the angle at which to hold the cane and the amount of pressure required to burst it at the first attempt. Then try the manoeuvre from your pony's back, which will help to get your pony used to having balloons popping around his feet. What you should be aiming at is being able to gallop past a line of balloons and burst one without checking your speed.

## Fishing Race

This is a race where the rider has to retrieve wooden fish from a bin by means of a cane with a hook on the end which attaches to a ring in the nose of each fish. The 'catch' then has to be hung on a crossbar fitted with hooks at the far end of the arena. In individual games the fish have to be hung out by the rider, an action which she will usually be allowed to carry out by hand. Clearly a certain amount of precision is required to get the hook into the ring and you will not be able to do this while your pony is on the move. Concentrate, therefore, on making your pony stand absolutely still, and make up time by galloping between the items of equipment. Once hooked, the fish is unlikely to fall off the 'rod' as you gallop from the bin to the crossbar.

## Flag Race

The flag in this race usually consists of a triangular pennant attached to one end of a 4-foot cane. Provided you hold the flag like a sword, you should have no difficulty in inserting it into a cut-down cone. The hardest part of the race is collecting a single flag from several in a cone, especially if they are bunched together. It is important to remove only one flag, so you should decide mentally which one to take before you even reach the cone. It may be necessary to check the speed of your pony as you approach the flags.

Where a single flag in a cone has to be collected, the danger is that in grasping and removing the flag you accidentally knock over the cone. It is essential to pick up the flag and flick it backwards in one movement as your pony gallops past the cone. Practise at home inserting the flag and picking it up again.

## Hi-Lo

Tennis balls balanced on cones have to be transferred one by one from the cones to a net mounted on a post about 7 feet above the ground: hence the name Hi-Lo, although lo-hi might describe the action more accurately. As with the Ball and Cone Race, described earlier, extreme care is needed when collecting the ball. When depositing the ball in the net, the closer you can get to the net the less likely you are to drop the ball. Practise standing in your stirrups and reaching high above your head (this is a good exercise for getting you fit). Try to carry out the manoeuvre without stopping your pony completely.

Get in close to the net and stand up in the stirrups to place the ball successfully in the Hi-Lo race

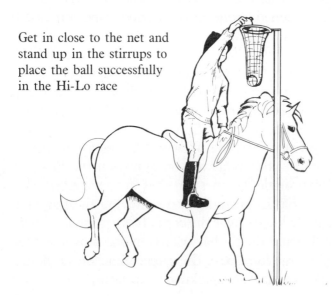

## Hurdle Race

This is not a jumping race for your pony but one in which you have to dismount, pass under high hurdles and over low ones, remount and ride to the finish, or to the next rider if it is a team game. It is not usually used for individual games because of the difficulty of keeping hold of your pony while you are crawling under the high hurdle. In team games, your pony will be held by your partner. Basically, this is a mounting and dismounting race, which is where practising comes in. You should also practise diving under a bar without touching it. In the race itself the manoeuvre is often made more difficult by the presence of a mug balanced on the high hurdle, which will fall if you bump against the bar.

## Knickerbocker Glory

Here you have to carry a lightweight plastic ball in an 'ice cream cone' up and down a line of bending poles. The 'ice cream cone' is the top part of a road cone, the bottom half being used for flag races. This can be quite a fast race, provided you can concentrate on keeping the ball in the cone, so practise your neck-reining as you will have only one hand with which to control and guide your pony.

## Litter Race

The skill in this race lies in being able to pick up a piece of litter on the end of a cane without having to check

59

In the race itself the manoeuvre is often made more difficult
by the presence of a mug balanced on the high hurdle

your pony. It requires plenty of practice at home, at first starting slowly and then building up speed as you get more proficient. The secret is to hold the cane about half-way along its length, to approach the litter with its open end towards you and to bend as low as you can when inserting the point of the cane into the litter. As soon as it is safely in, bring the cane up sharply (but not too sharply for fear of flicking the litter off the cane). Always use the forward momentum of your pony to help you in the manoeuvre.

## Moat and Castle

This involves transferring a tennis ball from a bucket of water to a cone. There may be more than one tennis ball and more than one cone but you have to be supple enough to be able to bend right down to the bucket. Unless you can get your hand underneath the tennis ball, you will have to dismount to retrieve it, clearly a disadvantage if your opponents can grab the ball without getting off. Placing the ball on the cone at the far end is easier than in the Ball and Cone Race because you are circling the cone as you carry out the action. It is a race which needs a great deal of practice.

## Mug Race

The various mug races in popular use all require the rider to place a mug on the top of a pole. Speed relies on galloping between the poles and tight turns, but make certain that you do not slam the mug down on to the pole or it will bounce off as soon as you let go of it. Concentrate on placing the mug gently into position.

## Pony Club Race

Eight letters painted on to squares of plywood or cardboard have to be collected two at a time from a table and hung on a frame so that they spell out words. There are therefore two skills required in this game, the manual skill of hooking the letters into position and the intellectual skill of putting them into the right place. Both skills will improve with practice. Make certain that your pony will stand still on command. Most errors occur when the letters are being hung on the hooks.

## Post Office Race

Envelopes, fastened to the tops of bending poles with rubber bands, have to be collected and posted into a cardboard box through a slit in the lid. The envelopes can be snatched at speed – remember to keep your eye on each one – but precision is needed when inserting it into the slot. The game is easier if the post box is placed on top of a bin or bucket, but be prepared to have to bend right down if it is on the ground. The same degree of suppleness will be needed as in the Ball and Bucket or Moat and Castle Races. Practise controlling your pony with one hand as you make a tight turn.

## Ring Race

This is another race where items of equipment have to be transferred from one place to another. The items in this case are rubber vacuum cleaner rings suspended in pairs from a crossbar at one end of the arena which have to be placed on a large hook mounted on a bending pole. Success depends on getting between the crossbar and the bending pole as quickly as possible but having sufficient control of your pony to pick up the rings without dropping them. Your pony should slow down sufficiently to make the task easier but be ready to spring back into a gallop as soon as the manoeuvre is over.

## Stepping Stone Dash

The ability to dismount and mount quickly and having a pony which leads willingly are essential to this race. The rider has to negotiate a line of stepping stones halfway up the arena whilst holding only the reins of the pony. If you step off or miss a stone you have to cross the whole line again. You are not allowed to get a 'lift' from the pony by leaning on him or using him to steady yourself. Practise running along a row of bricks, and make certain that your vault is accurate.

## Sword Race

The rings required for this race are difficult to make at home and for this reason the game is rarely found

63

in gymkhana schedules. However, it is a popular choice at Prince Philip Cup competitions at Zone level because, performed well, it is fast and spectacular. The object of the race is to collect large metal rings attached to the tops of bending poles by means of a sword. The rings must not be allowed to fall to the ground. In team races, each rider in turn collects a ring before handing over the sword to the next rider. The last rider, therefore, already has three rings on her sword before she attempts to spear the fourth. Individual competitors have to collect four rings as they gallop from one end of the line to the other.

Sureness of eye and good co-ordination are important qualities in this event, as it is very easy to misjudge the sword-thrust when travelling fast. Keep the point of the sword very slightly higher than the hilt when spearing the rings; otherwise they may slip off.

## LUCK EVENTS

Where luck plays a large part in a race, no practising is necessary. The two most popular luck events are **Crossing the River** and **Coloured Corners.** In the first, riders have to follow one another across the 'river', formed by laying two jumping poles on the ground about 10 to 12 yards apart. When the music stops or a whistle or hooter is sounded, anyone caught in the river is out. You can minimise the time spent in the river by stepping up your speed as you pass through it, but it is still mainly a matter of luck if you make it to the final six.

Coloured Corners is even more of a chancy affair. Each corner of the arena is given a colour, identified by a coloured flag or balloon. At a signal, competitors go to one of the corners which may not necessarily be the one they were approaching when the music stopped. A coloured ball or counter is drawn from a hat and all riders in the corner which corresponds to the counter are out.

**Shoe Scramble** is a game sometimes chosen by organisers as a means of giving less experienced competitors a chance of winning a rosette. Several different shoes are hidden in a pile of straw. Each rider is given a shoe and has to find its partner in the straw. As soon as she has a pair, she remounts her pony and rides to the finish.

# Chapter Four

# PRACTISING RINGCRAFT

This is the art of being in the right place at the right time. Winning competitors have ringcraft developed to a high degree.

The skill also includes knowing how to treat your pony. Many riders forget, in the excitement of taking part in games competitions, that their ponies are living creatures which must be treated with consideration if they are to give of their best.

## Warming-up

It is perfectly reasonable to give your pony a little warming-up exercise when you arrive at a show, especially if he has been standing in a trailer. It is not reasonable to ride around between races, which will serve only to tire the pony.

## Watering

Never give your pony a drink of water in between races

66

... ponies are living creatures which must be treated with
consideration if they are to give of their best

or before you go into the ring. The time to offer him water is at least half an hour before your first event or after he has finished all the races in which he is taking part.

## Collecting ring

While you are at a show, listen to announcements. Competitors are usually asked to go to the collecting ring when an event is due to begin. Play fair in the collecting ring. The steward often has a shrewd idea of who are the best competitors and may sometimes try to get the six strongest into one heat. Never argue. If you really want to avoid competing in a heat with your friend or with the county champion, the best way is not to stand alongside them. Make sure you know where they are in the collecting ring and simply move away. Remember that no more than six riders can form one heat.

## In the ring

To give yourself the best chance of coming out best in a tight finish, choose the lane *furthest* from the judges. Unless the judge is sitting on a flat trailer so that he is higher than the competitors, he will almost always place the further riders in front of those nearest to him.

Before a race begins, ask how many riders will qualify for the final. There is no point in riding your pony flat out to win your heat if you can still reach the final by coming second or even third. Qualifiers are usually asked to wait in a corner of the ring; this is the time to dismount and give your pony a rest. He will need all his strength and stamina for the final. Remember that in a race with a great many competitors, you may have to take part in a semi-final as well as a heat. If you have entered, say, six classes, this could mean taking part in as many as eighteen races during the afternoon.

## Reins

Short reins give you close control of your pony. If your reins are long, tie a knot in them so that, when the reins are slack, the knot lies about 12 inches (30 cm) in front

Knot in the reins to give closer control. The reins should be short enough for the knot to rest on the crest well in front of the withers

If your pony has a very long mane pull it to a neat and tidy
even length

of the withers. This also helps to keep the loop of the reins out of the way of your feet and legs. If your pony has a very long mane and you do not intend to show him in 'Mountain and Moorland' classes, pull the mane to a neat and tidy even length. This will prevent you from getting the reins tangled in the mane while you are handling or carrying equipment. Plaiting, as an alternative, is not permitted in Pony Club mounted games competitions.

## Objections

Only object if you are confident that there has been a clear breach of the rules, such as a rider who is over age or a pony which is too big or too small. If you are sure of your facts, you should make the complaint in writing to the secretary and pay the necessary deposit.

Never, ever, complain that something is unfair. Judges sometimes make mistakes, but it is very difficult for them to put things right in the middle of an event. They are unlikely to run the race again – such an action would indeed be unfair to those who are not involved in a dispute. It is better for your reputation as a gymkhana competitor to take a philosophical view and accept the judge's decision. After all, another time, it could be in your favour.

Above all, be a good loser and a generous winner.

# Chapter Five

# TIPS ON TEAMWORK

Joining a team-training squad is one of the best ways of improving your gymkhana technique. The discipline imposed by having to attend regular practices and by working with other riders is invaluable. Criticism within the squad is nearly always constructive, and a strongly competitive attitude – so essential to the art of winning as opposed to merely taking part – is built up within the members of a squad as they vie with each other to make the first team.

The biggest bonus of all, however, is the development of team spirit. While it is not necessarily true to say that a team is only as good as its weakest member, it is not as easy to carry a passenger as it might be in many other team games.

Members of a team which has been together for some time get to know one another very well, understand each other's moods, appreciate when to support and encourage and when to tease or criticise. They soon learn that no one is perfect, no one can turn in a faultless

72

performance every time and if it is not you who makes a mistake today it could very well be your turn tomorrow.

In a team, there is always someone who can take you to one side and help you to iron out your weaknesses. Perhaps you are uncertain of your vault, possibly you find it difficult not to knock the cone over every time you grab a flag, maybe it is the bottle race which fills you with apprehension: whatever your problem others have suffered similarly in the past and learned how to overcome their difficulties.

Many riders find that they prefer team competitions to individual events. If asked why, they will answer, 'Because they're more fun'. Usually what they mean is that the preparation beforehand is all part of the enjoyment – the build-up, the sense of belonging, the feeling that you all want to do well, to be a credit to your branch, your county or your trainer.

The opportunity to take part in team events has never been greater. For the under-fifteens, the Pony Club mounted games provides a wide array of inter-branch contests, headed, of course, by the championships but spreading out to include friendly competitions of all types, from demonstration, invitation-only contests at county agricultural shows to novice team events for the under-twelves.

For those who have enjoyed their Prince Philip Cup years and are loath to abandon the friendship and fun when they reach the grand old age of fifteen, the Mounted Games Association of Great Britain offers them an extension. The Association was formed a few years ago with just that object in mind, and teams are organised on a county basis. Members are eligible up to the age of twenty-one, and with all the experience that most of the riders have packed into their mounted games careers, the county competitions are fast and furious, with ponies and riders displaying quite extraordinary gymkhana skills.

With both the Pony Club and the MGAGB, the team events for the coming season are chosen early on in the year to give team trainers time to assemble the equipment. In both organisations, the selected events are very similar although they may have different names: the Pony Club's 'team bending', for example, is no different from the MGAGB's 'speed weaving'. There are some twenty or so games from which the selection is made and, while the ruling committees do try to introduce new games from time to time, the innovations are usually variations on an old theme.

Whatever programme of events is chosen, this will form the basis of any inter-branch or inter-county competitions during the season. It would be a very foolish organiser who tried to hold a team competition with a totally random selection of games.

## Overcoming problems

When you practise on your own, with the intention of entering gymkhanas as an individual, you are training your pony for events which are performed differently from those designed for teams. There is little difference in handling equipment, but many games for individuals require you to ride up and down the arena, transferring flags or balls or mugs from one place to another. Your pony learns to stop and turn in the centre of the arena, making the journey to the far end two or three times before galloping to the finish. Team members, on the other hand, usually have to perform an action only once, perhaps collecting an item on the way up, depositing it at the top and returning to the base line at full speed.

It is noticeable that ponies which have been used only for team competitions tend to flounder when entered in an individual event. They are so used to getting back to the start line as quickly as possible that they tend to fight the rider if asked to vary their usual action. Some ponies, in fact, find it very difficult to adapt and their riders must decide whether they prefer to be team specialists or individual competitors.

A team pony must, above all, be capable of acting with other ponies. They should be willing to lead and be led, stand their ground when faced with another pony approaching fast from the front and never jib or nap when a rider is scrambling to mount or a second rider is looking for a lift.

In team competitions, a quick, clean handover of equipment is vital to the team's success. If a waiting pony backs off or dances sideways at the approach of an incoming pony, the handover is likely to be fumbled. The moment that one piece of equipment passes from one rider's hand to the next is the very moment when both riders should be able to concentrate totally on the exchange. If one rider is struggling to control her pony and keep him in position, she cannot watch the other rider's hand with all her attention. One piece of dropped equipment may mean failure to reach the final. Consistently winning teams achieve success through their own skill, not through other people's mistakes.

**Backing-off** is a common problem with an inexperienced pony. A pony has a wide field of lateral vision but a permanent blind spot just in front of him. Unlike humans he cannot see the end of his own nose. An incoming pony enters the blind spot just before the moment of handover, and it is the most natural thing in the world for the pony to take a step or two backwards. Experienced ponies have learned to trust their riders at this point and will turn their heads slightly in order to bring the second pony back into vision.

If your pony runs backwards at the handover, try to make it as difficult as possible for him to react in this way The best way to achieve this is to make sure that he is actually moving *forwards* at the vital moment. So keep your pony well back from the changeover line and start walking towards the line as the incoming pony approaches you. It is very difficult for a pony to change direction – from going forwards to going backwards – quickly enough to disturb the handover, especially if you keep your legs on firmly and relax pressure on the bit. Even if he tries, he will still have to stop before altering direction and, so long as you get your timing right, you will have the piece of equipment safely in your hand before he takes one step in reverse.

If a waiting pony dances sideways at the approach of an
oncoming pony, the handover is likely to be fumbled

Another common problem at handover time is when the pony **shies** or **swerves** to one side. In this circumstance the forward movement will not help. The sidestep he makes may not be very great but it can still be enough to carry your outstretched hand out of range of the other rider's. In most cases the answer is constant practice. To begin with, it can help to position the steadiest pony in your squad alongside your own pony, thus preventing any sideways attempt. This pony must be absolutely rock-solid; most squads have at least one and the steadying influence such a pony can have on the others is invaluable. But in a competition the rules forbid any pony not involved in the changeover from standing on the changeover line, so eventually you will have to practise without the anchor pony in attendance.

Steady but constant repetition will, with luck, overcome both these behavioural problems in the end. The incoming pony should always, at the beginning, approach slowly (if necessary at a walk), only building up speed as the nervous pony relaxes.

If, however, in spite of patience and perseverance, your pony is still too apprehensive to accept a handover cleanly, the only solution is to be the first rider to go. For some reason, few ponies deviate from the line when they return to the start; the problems are almost always confined to the waiting pony.

**Approaching a dismounted rider** can cause problems with some ponies. The rider may be standing alone, waiting to hand equipment to her team-mate (as happens in Postman's Chase) or holding a frame or gallows on which something has to be hung (Fishing Race, Pony Club Race, Ring Race). But the pony really dislikes coming close enough for his rider to carry out the action required. He hesitates, naps, may even wheel round and try to gallop back down the arena.

This situation is another which calls for patience and gentle persuasion. The rock-steady pony could help here, accompanying your pony up to the person on the ground, showing him that there is nothing to be afraid of, no gremlins lurking, no lions or leopards waiting to pounce. Sometimes the solution is simple; the dismounted rider merely has to turn her back or, instead of approaching the gallows head on, you come towards it at a different angle. If, however, all methods fail, then you must accept the situation; for this particular race your pony must be the one which drops out.

**Leading and being led** feature in several team races (Groom's Race, Stepping Stone Dash, Tyre Race, etc.). Leading problems usually involve the riderless pony, which dislikes being hauled along by his rein and tends to hang back. Unfortunately, the more he hangs back the more the problem is compounded until finally the rider holding the rein is forced to let go or be pulled off the back of her own pony.

To overcome the problem, practise with your partner not only at formal training sessions but also when you are out hacking together. Get your partner to hold your pony's rein while you are still in the saddle and able to push him forward with your legs. When he is quite happy to walk alongside the other pony, step up the pace until he is leading easily at all speeds. The next stage is to jump off your pony, leaving him to be led along by your partner. If possible, jump off at a brisk trot or canter; this is, after all, exactly what you have to do in the Stepping Stone Dash and the Tyre Race. If your training has gone well, your pony should have forgotten all his old reluctance and be quite happy to match his stride to the other pony's.

After that, use the training sessions to practise the leading technique with different ponies. By that time, your pony should be able to accompany any pony at any pace and be willing to be led from either side.

**Fear of flags** is not uncommon. Sometimes the pony dislikes the flapping of the flags and flatly refuses to approach the cone containing them. The fear can eventually be overcome by showing the pony that there is nothing to worry about. Start by standing on the ground, holding a flag and talking to the pony in a gentle, encouraging voice. Let him sniff it, all the time stroking him quietly and talking to him. Take the flag in your hand and get on, if necessary furling the material so that it no longer flaps, and ride round with the cane in your hand. Hand it to other riders and get them to hand it to you. Always keep calm yourself and, if your relationship with your pony is a good one, he should soon be treating flags with a lofty disdain.

A similar approach is needed if your pony dislikes canes being waved or picked up. Show him that a cane offers as little threat as any other item of equipment and he will soon come to accept it.

... your pony should soon be treating flags with a lofty disdain

# Chapter Six

# EQUIPMENT FOR PRACTISING

When you join a mounted games squad, you have access to all the equipment you are likely to need. The average games trainer gathers together all manner of bits and pieces in the course of training teams, but this should not stop you from starting a collection yourself, particularly as this will give you the chance to practise on your own or with one or two friends. Most equipment can be acquired quite cheaply, especially if you are good at woodwork and have the tools available to help you. You will find all the advice you need in this chapter, which not only describes all the items of equipment in common use at gymkhanas, but also explains how to make them.

## Bending poles

The best bending poles are broom-handles. They are the right length, reasonably robust and cost about a pound each. You will need enough to give you a practice lane of five poles, plus spares in case of breakages. If you sharpen the points, they can be knocked into the ground when setting up the lane. Alternatively, since regular banging with a club hammer inevitably shortens the life of a bending pole, it makes sense to buy metal spikes with crosspieces for treading them into the ground. Each pole can be permanently fixed to a spike and it then takes only a matter of seconds to set it up. To give the poles added durability, seal them with varnish or paint.

If you can afford to spend more initially, ready-made poles can be bought from a company called QML (see the Useful Addresses section at the end of the book for the full name and address). These poles come complete with spikes, and the company also supply heavy metal bases into which the spikes can be slotted. These are useful when bending poles have to be set up in an arena with an all-weather surface, which could be damaged by spikes being driven into it.

With a little time and effort it is possible to weight the bottom of the poles yourself. Collect old paint tins or instant coffee cans, catering size. Stud the bottom 4 inches (10 cm) of each pole with flat-headed galvanised nails, placed at intervals so that the nails stick out about three-quarters of an inch (2 cm). Stand the pole, nail end downwards, upright in the centre of the tin and half fill the container with a sand and cement mortar mix (use one part cement to three parts sand, blended with water). Leave to dry.

The result of this work is a weighted pole which can

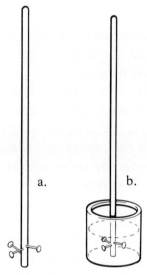

Making a bending pole
a. Bang nails into the base of
the pole
b. Stand the pole in a catering
can half filled with concrete and
leave to dry

a.

b.

be stood directly on the ground. On an uneven surface the poles may not be very stable, but they are quite effective in a bark or sand arena.

If broom-handles are too expensive, buy 1-inch square softwood from a timber merchant and cut it into 4-foot (120 cm) lengths. Be sure to varnish or paint the poles to make them last.

## Cones

These are a first-class investment even if you give up mounted games in the future. They have so many uses – as markers for dressage and arenas, fillers for jumps, warning signs for hazards like rabbit holes on a cross-country course. They can be bought, expensively, from shops specialising in equestrian products, but the cheapest source is a builders' merchant, especially those which stock road-mending tools and equipment.

Cones come in two basic sizes – a standard 18 inch (45 cm) model and the much larger version often seen on motorways. The standard size is the one used for mounted games.

A brand new cone usually has a sealed top or at best

Cut off just below the top to give a cone suitable for the Ball and Cone Race or to support a bending pole for practising

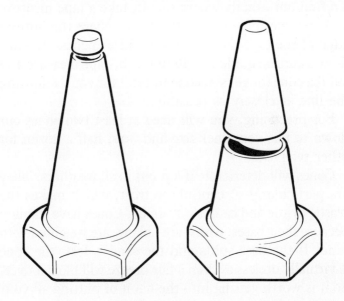

Cut off the top half of the cone to provide
a suitable flag container

a very small hole the size of a five pence coin, so the first thing you have to do is cut the top off. The best tool for this job is a Stanley knife fitted with a new blade, with which you can cut through the plastic all round the cone just below the top. (Get someone to cut it for you if you haven't used a Stanley knife before.) The resulting cone can now be used for balancing a tennis ball on. It can also be used in bending to support a broom-handle pole.

Cones for flag containers should be cut off much lower down. Pony Club mounted games rules stipulate that the opening should be 4 inches (10 cm) in diameter. To find out exactly where to cut, take a tape measure and encircle the cone: at the point where the bottom edge of the tape measure shows 12½ inches (32 cm), draw a cutting guideline. Remove the tape measure and cut the cone (or get someone to cut it for you), following the line as closely as possible.

For practising, you will need at least two cones cut down to flag container size and, say, half a dozen for other purposes.

Cones will deteriorate if left out in all weathers. They are particularly susceptible to frost, which makes the plastic brittle and causes it to crack. Cones have stability because their bases, which are hollow, are weighted with sand. If the base splits and the sand is lost, the cone is virtually useless as even a fair breeze will blow it over. So it is worth getting into the habit of putting all your practice equipment carefully away when you have finished using it; it will then last for years.

## Canes

The cane used for most purposes measures 4 feet (120 cm) in length and is made of bamboo. It is widely available at gardening centres. Always bind the ends of the cane with insulating tape to prevent splintering. Ordinary canes are used in the Litter Race, with pins taped to one end in the Balloon Bursting Race, and for mounting the flags used in the Flag Race.

## Flags

The flags used in Prince Philip competitions are either 9 inches (22.5 cm) square, or 9 inches wide if the flag is triangular. For practice purposes, smaller flags are perfectly adequate and there is no need to worry if the only fabric available to you is from the ragbag – you will need to make at least half a dozen.

The first thing to do is make a paper pattern. If you want to be really accurate, use graph paper for this purpose; otherwise, brown wrapping paper will do. Use reasonably strong paper so that the pattern can be used several times. Once you have made a template, pin it to the fabric and cut round the perimeter. With care, several thicknesses of fabric can be cut at the same time.

Make a wide hem along the staff edge and a narrow hem along the other two sides. Stitch across one end of the wide hem, so that it forms a sleeve. Insert the cane into the sleeve, pulling the flag well down. Secure it to the cane at the lower end with insulating tape.

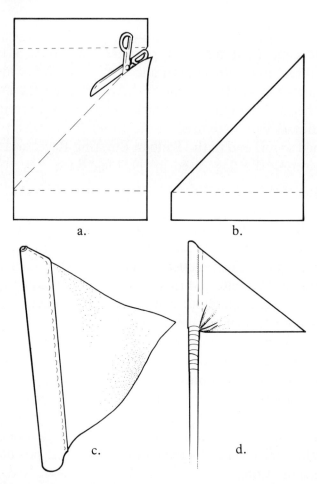

a.

b.

c.

d.

Making a flag
a. Cut along the dotted line to get two flags from one piece of fabric.
b. Fold over the hem at the dotted line
c. Stitch along the hem, leaving one end of the channel open as shown
d. Secure the flag to the cane by wrapping insulating tape
directly below

## Bottles

Ask your friends to save 1-litre squash bottles for you, which can be weighted by filling them a third full with sand. If you then add expanded polystyrene beads to the bottle before screwing the top back on you will greatly extend the life of the bottle (because of the flimsy nature of the plastic used in the construction of these bottles, they tend to split easily). Do not paint the bottles because this makes them very brittle. Paint should be used only if the whole surface has been covered in adhesive fabric tape first, but such refinements are not necessary with practice equipment.

a. Bottle filled with one-third sand, two-thirds polystyrene beads

b. Cut the top off a litre size washing-up bottle to produce first-class 'litter'

## Litter

When Litter Races were first introduced, all kinds of litter were recommended: boxes; juice cartons; washing-up liquid bottles; anything, in fact, which could be picked up on the end of a cane. Over the years, however, the washing-up liquid bottle has become the standard form of litter. The litre size is best and the bottle should be cut off at the shoulder, using a sharp knife (again, get someone to do this for you if you are not used to working with sharp tools). Try to collect as much litter as possible: ask your friends and neighbours to save their bottles for you as you will need at least five pieces of litter to match the number used in an actual race.

## Swords

The Sword Race does not crop up very often in gymkhanas but is a popular event at Zone Final level in the Pony Club Championship. To make a sword, you

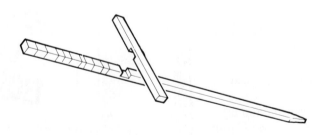

Fixing the crosspiece onto a simple wooden sword

will need a 4-foot (120 cm) length of 1-inch square softwood. Mark off 1 foot (30 cm) from one end and cut it in two at the mark. The shorter length forms the crosspiece and should be fixed across the longer section so that the blade is 2 feet (60 cm) long and the hilt 1 foot (30 cm) (see the illustration on p.90). Use a plane to taper the blade and to round off all sharp edges. Finish by sandpapering smooth and bind the hilt with coloured insulating tape.

## Rings

Two types of rings are used in gymkhana events. The ones for the Sword Race are not easy to make yourself unless you have access to metal-working tools, but you can make a cardboard template which any blacksmith will copy and cut out for you from sheet metal. For practising the Sword Race, you will need four such rings, each with an external diameter of 6 inches (15 cm) and a hole in the middle of 4 inches (10 cm) diameter. A short straight piece projects from the ring so that it

Two types of ring

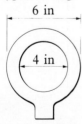

a. Metal ring with stem for the Sword Race

b. Vacuum cleaner ring covered with insulating tape for the Ring Race

can be attached to the top of a bending pole with a rubber band (see the illustration on p.91).

For the Ring Race you will need the rubber rings used in vacuum cleaners, which are easily obtainable from electrical shops. You will need several for practising and they should be bound in coloured insulating tape to make them easier to see.

**Gallows**

The Fishing Race, the Ring Race and the Pony Club Race all require a frame or gallows on which the fish, rings or letters can be hung. The first two need a T-

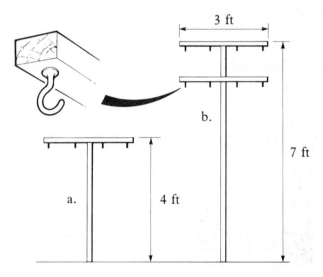

a. The 4-foot high gallows used in the Fishing Race and the Ring Race    b. The taller gallows used in the Pony Club Race

shaped frame, 4 feet (120 cm) high, with cup-hooks fitted to the underside of the crosspiece. The frame required for the Pony Club Race is taller – 7 feet (210 cm) high – with two crossbars, one at the top and another 12 inches (30 cm) below it. Four hooks are attached to the underside of each bar. For both types of frame, the crosspiece is 3 feet (90 cm) long, and the frames are made from 1 × 2 inch softwood.

In a team competition, the gallows are held upright by a dismounted member of the team, but if you are practising on your own, you may find it easier to sharpen the base of the upright to a point so that it can be driven into the ground. Alternatively, sink a fencing post into the ground (which can then be left there permanently) and lash the frame to the post whenever you want to practise.

## Sacks

Try to get hold of a hessian sack so that you can practise the Sack Race. These are not easy to come by nowadays as most foodstuffs are supplied in paper sacks, but it is worth asking a local corn chandler if he has a hessian sack for sale. Make certain to dry it out if it gets wet during practice; it will deteriorate and rot if you put it away wet.

The sack used for Postman's Chase is much smaller than the traditional hessian one, being only 15 inches (42.5 cm) wide by 24 inches (60 cm) long. It does not have to be of hessian but can be made of any cotton material – an old pillowcase will do.

... the gallows are held upright by a dismounted member of
the team

## Letters

The letters for Postman's Chase are best cut out of hardboard. They should be envelope-shaped, 8 inches (20 cm) by 4 inches (10 cm), with the corners rounded off. The Pony Club letters are 8 inches (20 cm) square, with the appropriate characters (P, O, N, Y, C, L, U, B) painted on or drawn on with a marker pen. Since you have to screw in a small ring to the top of each letter, you might find it easier to make the letters out of plywood.

## Socks

Collect as many old socks as you can and stuff the toes with screwed-up newspaper. Then roll each sock up, turn over the top and oversew the open ends so that they cannot come undone. If possible, choose brightly coloured socks because they are easier to see when placed on the ground – quite important in the Sock Race!

## Useful Extras

Anything which might come in handy for practising is worth storing away. Old tennis racquets, tennis balls, batons made from 12-inch (30 cm) lengths of broom-handle, pieces of rope 3 feet (90 cm) long for the Rope Race, motor cycle tyres, metal mugs and plastic beakers – these will all be useful.

The Balloon Race requires a holder for the balloons and this can be made from a piece of fabric about 4 feet

(120 cm) long by 12 inches (30 cm) wide. Sew clothes pegs at intervals down the centre of the cloth and a loop at each corner. The cloth can then be secured in place by passing meat skewers through the loops and tapping them into the ground. Inflated balloons are attached to the cloth by means of the clothes pegs.

Large flower pots can be used for the Stepping Stone Dash, but if these are hard to come by bricks will do instead.

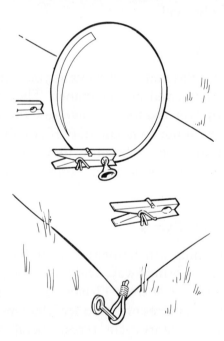

Fabric holder for practising the Balloon Race, secured to the ground by skewers

# Chapter Seven

# DRESS AND SADDLERY

The rules governing what you and your pony should wear for competitions are set out quite specifically in the Pony Club's mounted games rule book. Nevertheless, in ordinary gymkhanas and other team contests you should always read the schedule carefully to make certain that there are no unforeseen regulations.

## DRESS

### Prince Philip Cup

Light-coloured jodhpurs and jodhpur boots must be worn at all competitions, although breeches and boots are permitted at Area Meetings and Zone Finals. These should be worn with white shirts with long sleeves, Pony Club ties and tabards or bibs in the team colours. The hat must conform to British Standard BS4472 and bear the BSI kitemark label with 4472 printed on it.

... you should always read the schedule carefully to make
certain that there are no unforeseen regulations

If it does not have this label, the rider will not be allowed to compete. The hat must have a black or dark blue cover and must be worn with the chinstrap fastened whenever the rider is mounted.

In cold or wet weather, a rider may wear a white V-necked acrylic sweater with long sleeves over the shirt and/or a transparent colourless or white cagoule, also with long sleeves.

## Other Competitions

The rules tend to be much more relaxed at gymkhanas, although show organisers usually insist on the wearing of BS4472 hats with chinstraps fastened. Short-sleeved shirts, even T-shirts, are often permitted on a hot day, although you might be turned out of the ring if you appeared in a bikini top! Jeans are usually discouraged (in fact, they are very uncomfortable for riding), but will not necessarily disbar you from competing. No one will object if you wear a riding jacket or even an anorak, but you could find that these are a disadvantage in mounted games because they can restrict your movements. Jerseys or sweat shirts are the most popular form of clothing for gymkhanas.

Sensible footwear is best. Jodhpur boots are the wisest choice as they are comfortable, safe and more flexible than riding boots. Other footwear, such as trainers, gymshoes and wellington boots, may be permitted by some organisers, but your own common sense should tell you not to wear them as they are not safe for riding.

Nobody will stop you from wearing gloves, but they can be a definite handicap in mounted games where dexterity in handling equipment is so important.

In ordinary gymkhanas, it is a good idea to wear a jersey or sweat shirt that is brightly coloured; in a close finish, you are more likely to be noted and remembered by a judge trying to sort out contenders. This is not cheating but a sensible form of gamesmanship.

## SADDLERY

### Prince Philip Cup

General purpose saddles, made on a conventional tree, should be well fitting and in good condition. Pad saddles without a tree or with a half-tree or front arch only are not allowed. The stirrup bars should have the safety clips open. Racing saddles shorter than 16 inches in length and weighing less than 5 pounds are prohibited.

Stirrup leathers must be well maintained, with no signs of cracking or broken stitching. The irons should be of normal hunting type, not lightweight racing irons, although safety stirrups are permitted. The girths must have two buckles.

Snaffle bridles are the only type permitted, worn with a plain snaffle bit which has a straight bar or a single joint. The mouthpiece must be smooth all round. No other type of bit is allowed, and all bitless bridles are banned.

Martingales may be worn, but only the standing, running, bib or Irish type, and only one may be used at any one time. The standing martingale must be attached to the cavesson part of the noseband. Drop nosebands, including the grakle and flash, are allowed but the Kineton is not. A running martingale may not be used as a standing one.

The leatherwork of the bridle must be in good condition, with no frayed or broken stitching. The reins may be rubber-covered or plaited to improve grip and may be knotted when in use to reduce their length.

Stirrup irons and bits made of stainless steel are preferred. The use of nickel bits and irons, whilst not actually banned, is discouraged because their brittleness make them dangerous.

At all major Pony Club team competitions, and at many inter-branch friendlies as well, a tack inspection is carried out. Riders with ill-fitting or unsafe tack will be told that they cannot take part until the tack is changed to the satisfaction of the Official Steward. Once a pony and rider have passed the scrutiny of the tack inspection judges, the saddlery or dress cannot be changed and competitors will be checked in the collecting ring to make certain that this rule is being observed.

Any tack not allowed in the competition cannot be used outside the arena at any time during the day.

## Other Competitions

As with dress, the rules governing saddlery tend to be much more relaxed. Nevertheless, riders should always check the schedule carefully to make sure that they do not fall foul of any local rule. If in doubt, it is sensible to telephone the organiser beforehand to get an instant ruling.

Most gymkhanas, in fact, permit the use of a Pelham bit and some will allow hackamores. The Pelham, because of its curb action, is a more severe bit than the snaffle, but some ponies do go better and are more controllable with a curb chain. Pad saddles are rarely banned from ordinary gymkhanas.

A good gymkhana judge, however, should notice if tack is ill fitting, and while it is unlikely that a rider will be turned out of the ring she may well be warned about the offending item and told to get something done about it before the next show. This most usually applies to saddles which are down on the withers when the rider is mounted.

If you think that your saddle is unlikely to pass a judge's scrutiny, do get something done about it straightaway. Quite apart from the risk of being disqualified, such a saddle could be causing your pony discomfort if not actual pain. At worst, it may set up problems which could take a long time to clear up and lead to your pony being out of commission just when you need him most, i.e. throughout the gymkhana season. Any reputable saddler will advise you on the fitting of your pony's saddle and if necessary will re-stuff it. A broken tree, however, cannot be repaired and the saddle must be replaced.

Keeping your tack clean and in good repair makes

sense. Few people really enjoy cleaning tack, although it is one of those activities which are more fun if you can carry it out in company. You should try to get into the habit of giving both saddle and bridle a thorough clean at least once a week, always checking it carefully for signs of wear. Use a good quality saddle soap or leather cleaner (which also feeds the leather) and avoid putting it away encrusted with mud and grease.

Even where you use a webbing bridle for everyday riding and practice, keeping your leather one for competitions, remember to inspect your leather bridle from time to time. Depending on where it is stored, it can easily dry out (causing cracking) or develop mould. Metalwork (bits and irons) should be washed in hot, soapy water, rinsed carefully and dried.

## Pre-competition Inspections

In the Pony Club team contests, separate rosettes are usually awarded for turn-out. This means that the ponies and riders are inspected as well as tack. It is more important for both you and your pony to be tidy and clean, with good well-fitting tack, than for the team to appear with such gimmicks as matching browbands and saddle cloths. Admittedly, these do make the team look smart and eye-catching, and there is nothing wrong with them as long as everything else passes muster, but they are not vital.

Judges are aware that most gymkhana ponies live out and they would not expect you to remove a pony's natural protective grease, but you would lose marks if

Judges are aware that most gymkhana ponies live out, but
you would lose marks if your pony had any dried mud
clinging to him

your pony had any dried mud clinging to him. Check such areas as under the mane, around the ears and dock and under the belly. Ponies do not have to be shod but feet should be properly trimmed and picked out. Shoes, if worn, should fit properly, with clenches hammered down and no growth of hoof over the edges of the shoe. Dried mucus around the eyes and nostrils should be sponged away.

Manes do not have to be plaited but can be pulled. If you trim the mane behind the ears where the headpiece of the bridle rests, or just in front of the saddle, make certain that it has been trimmed properly. In the summer, fetlock feather can be trimmed with scissors but leave it intact in winter because it protects the feet.

Carry out a critical inspection of your pony before you enter the ring. Your team trainer will no doubt do the same thing but you should know what points to look for. Items that are sometimes overlooked are buckle guards, keepers on bridles, dried saddle soap in spare holes and wrinkled skin under girths.

Make certain that you, too, are as neat and tidy as possible. Pay attention to your collar, which can get tucked up, your hair (if you wear a hairnet, ensure that no tendrils are escaping) and the cleanliness of your boots. Finally, remember to *smile*. Judges are affected by the sight of a row of sullen faces, so however nervous you may be feeling – and it is a rare competitor who never suffers from nerves – hide it behind a cheerful countenance.

## Whips and Spurs

These are always banned, whatever gymkhana competition you enter. In any case, a good games pony should not need artificial aids. Remember that this rule also applies to the jumping competitions known as Chase Me Charlie and Barrel Elimination, both of which are classed as gymkhana events. If your pony will not jump without the help of a whip, you must either go back to the beginning in his schooling sessions or not enter such competitions at all.

# Chapter Eight

# THE DAY OF THE SHOW

After all the training and preparation you are ready to go to a show. If your pony is an all-rounder, you will find that most shows have a number of events that you can enter – jumping, working hunter pony, best rider, handy pony, turn-out, etc. – as well as gymkhana games. As a gymkhana specialist, your main difficulty will lie in choosing events in which you hope to do well but which will not tire either yourself or your pony before the gymkhana section begins.

You will also have to work out a timetable for the day. In shows where there is more than one ring, the schedule usually states the time the first event in each ring will begin but thereafter it is a matter of guesswork whether the events you want to enter will clash.

As a general rule, when calculating the time your event is likely to start, you should allow one hour for each showing class and about one and a half hours for every jumping class. This, of course, assumes a reasonable entry for the classes. Unfortunately you have no more idea than the organisers whether their show will be the popular one that weekend, or whether the showing judge is the sort who likes to look at every pony in detail or one who has made her mind up from the word go and is only going through the motions with the rest. The first kind will take the whole morning to come to a decision, while the second will be back in the refreshment tent before you have finished practising your bending.

The first intimation that a show is taking place is usually an advertisement in the local paper. Beware of assuming that the show you enjoyed last year will be held on the same weekend this year. Show organisers have a habit of changing both date and venue and there is no point in working out your plans for this year's season from last year's calendar.

Most advertisements give a brief resumé of the classes at the show, often in shortened form, such as SJ (Show Jumping), WHP (Working Hunter Pony), BR (Best Rider), TO (Turn-Out) and so on. Look for the shows which include gymkhana events in the advertisement. You will also be invited to send a stamped addressed envelope to the secretary. Do make certain that the envelope is big enough, especially if you are asking for more than one schedule. It is surprising how many riders think that a show secretary can cram six schedules into a minute pink envelope decorated with violets.

Schedules can also be picked up in saddlers' shops and from the secretary's tent or caterer's caravan at other shows.

As soon as you have the schedules make a note in your engagements diary or calendar of not only the date on which a show is taking place but also the day when the entries are due. It will save you a great deal of money if you can get your entries in on time. Entry forms are fairly standard in appearance and the information they require you to supply. There are columns for the class number, name of pony, name of rider and entry fee. Sometimes you are asked to give the height of the pony and the name of his owner. You will also be asked to write down your age and to fill in your name, address and telephone number.

There will usually be a request to send full remittance of entry fees with the entry form and the name of the person or event to which the cheque or postal order should be made out.

Sometimes there is space for you to sign the entry form together with a statement saying that you agree to abide by the rules of the show. The schedule will very likely have a paragraph disclaiming responsibility on the part of the organisers for any injury or accident which might befall you or your pony during the show. In general, this is a formality: the organisers through their public liability insurance would still be liable if you came to any harm through their negligence. It is perhaps worth remembering that all Pony Club events are automatically insured through the Pony Club and many open shows run by or on behalf of a Pony Club branch are similarly covered.

Once your entry form and fees have been sent off,

this is the last you will hear of them until the day of the show itself. Only the very big shows send you a receipt or acknowledgment. You should, however, make a note beside your diary entry of the show secretary's name and telephone number. Should there be a week of heavy rain just before the show or an outbreak of some infectious horse disease in your area, the show could be cancelled and it is important to know who to telephone for information. Remember that if the organisers cancel the show, you will get your entry fees returned. If, however, you decide at the last moment you would rather go up to London or take a trip to the beach, your entry fees will be forfeited. You will only get your money back if your pony falls sick or lame and you can send a vet's certificate to that effect. If *you* fall sick, even with a doctor's certificate, it is up to the organisers to decide whether your money will be refunded, although most secretaries in these circumstances would do so.

## Before the Show

Plan your programme before a show with care. You want your pony to be fit and full of life on the day of the show itself. Practise your gymkhana techniques regularly but never for too long and intersperse the games practice with other activities such as jumping (especially if you are also entering for jumping classes) and hacking. If the weather is very hot, try to arrange your practices for the early morning or early evening when the atmosphere is cooler and both you and your pony will enjoy the exercise.

Use fly repellent on your pony, sponging it on the areas most affected by flies: on the face and round the ears, under the belly, down the legs and around the dock. While the pony is in the field, put him in a headcollar with a fly fringe attached. A pony bothered by flies will use up a great deal of nervous energy trying to escape their attentions: you want to be able to harness that energy when you are taking part in competitions.

There are various factors which govern your plans for the eve of the show. The first is the time of your opening event, the second is your method of getting to the gymkhana. Less important but still capable of affecting your timetable are such things as the colour of your pony, what the weather appears to be like and whether you have a stable where you can keep him overnight.

In team competitions, particularly Pony Club ones where a turn-out and tack inspection is scheduled, your team trainer will be given the exact time your team's inspection will take place. It is important here to arrive at least an hour beforehand so that there is plenty of time to give the ponies their final polish and to check that all items of tack are clean, safe, sound and within the rules.

Organisers of these competitions usually plan the timetable to take into account the distance the teams have to travel. Even so, you may still find that you have to leave at six or seven in the morning. It is usually best for the whole team to travel together in one lorry: when the team members are all together on the journey, much of the pre-competition tension disappears and everyone arrives feeling relaxed and confident. If the lorry breaks down or anything else occurs to hold up progress, at least the team are together and a message may be sent to the competition organiser warning of a late arrival. Most organisers in this situation will rearrange the order of turn-out.

However, not all teams have the luxury of a single lorry and in most cases the members will be travelling separately. An individual entering the gymkhana classes at a show does not have other members of a team to think about, but the advice about arriving an hour beforehand still applies. Those who have entered only gymkhana classes will usually find that their first event is not due to start until the early afternoon. This gives them the luxury of having a whole morning in which to prepare for the show.

Most riders, however, do enter other events. Turn-out classes are always scheduled for the beginning of the show before plaits have had time to come undone or shoes become dusty. Showing and jumping classes tend to start with those for the younger competitors, the smaller ponies and the novice riders. You could well find yourself having to arrive at 8 a.m. and making an exceptionally early start in order to do so. It is clear, therefore, that most show preparation has to take place on the day before.

## On the Eve

If you have decided to give your pony a wash before the big day, remember that it is best to use shampoo only on the dirty areas. Your aim is to remove stains, not the essential oils and grease on the skin and in the coat which protect your pony from the weather. If you use a hosepipe, many ponies enjoy having it played gently over the body and this will help to remove surface dust.

Dry your pony carefully afterwards, paying particular attention to the legs and patting the heels as dry as you can. The best way to dry the tail is to grasp it at the bottom of the tail bone and swing the loose hairs round in a rapid circular movement. Afterwards put your pony in a sweat rug and wait until he is completely dry before turning him out again into the field.

Depending on your pony, it is usually better not to work him on the eve of the show. Some ponies, however, need to be exercised every day. If this is the case with yours, try to ride him early in the day, leaving the afternoon free for the washing session.

Always remember to inspect him carefully when you are grooming him, particularly his feet. New shoes should have been put on at least a week before the show, but if he did not need new shoes, check that no clenches have risen and that the shoes are still firmly in position. There is still time on the eve of the show for an emergency visit to or from the blacksmith.

Tack cleaning can be done in the early evening, and your own clothes should be cleaned, checked and laid out. Don't forget to clean the soles of your jodhpur boots!

Your pony can spend the night before the show in the stable if you have one. If the weather is warm and dry, however, it is better to leave him in the field. He may be dusty in the morning but he is unlikely to get any manure stains, always a risk in a stable. You should, of course, be confident that you can catch him.

Travelling to a show by trailer or lorry means that you can take a great deal of equipment with you. Grooming kit, water container, bucket, spare tack, changes of clothing for yourself, packed lunch, etc., can all be stored in the car or horsebox. At the show, the vehicle gives you a permanent base and a place in which your pony can stand out of the sun between events.

If your pony is a difficult loader, you must allow sufficient time to get him into the vehicle. Some ponies are only difficult if they have to travel alone. If your pony falls into that category, it is worthwhile taking your friend's pony along with yours, even if she is not intending to enter any classes. It could mean the difference between arriving on time with a happy, relaxed pony and reaching the showground late with a pony that is nervous and agitated and a rider in a state of collapse.

Planning your route a few days before with the help of a large-scale map is valuable, but road maps cannot show bottlenecks and roadworks, both of which could delay your journey, and few standard road maps indicate very steep hills. If possible, try to fit in a dry run, visiting the showground and noting possible hazards on the way. Remember that a car alone is much quicker than one with a trailer on the back, but the dry run at least gives you a chance to plan and explore detours.

With shows that are close to home, it is possible to hack to the show. Unless your parents are coming later in the car and can bring your equipment with them, you will have to carry it yourself. In this case, it is essential to confine your 'luggage' to the minimum: a headcollar (though this can be put on under your pony's bridle); a sweat rug; a hoofpick; possibly a water brush and a body brush and, last but not least, a packed lunch. For these you will need a rucksack so that your hands are free to control the pony when riding along the roads.

At a local show you are likely to know many of the other competitors. If the organisers have not provided somewhere shady for ponies without trailers to be tied up between events, you might try to team up with someone you know and share the facilities of her trailer.

Always allow plenty of time to get to the showground. It is better to walk the whole way than to have to hurry and tire your pony out before you have even arrived.

## At the Show

Having arrived at the show in good time make certain that your pony is settled and happy before going to the secretary's tent to pick up your number. If the show is already well under way, ask if it is running to time.

115

You will have to saddle and bridle your pony about half an hour before your first event and ride him round for a little to loosen him up. Riding round does not mean galloping up and down the field. Trot and canter a few orderly circles on both reins, practise your stops and starts and your vault.

When you are entering several events, be aware that there may be some time between each one. Make certain you know which ring you should be in and rest your pony between classes.

## The End of the Day

Try to clear up all your equipment and stow it into the car tidily. It is tempting just to hurl everything in higgledy-piggledy and sort it out when you get home, but if anything is missing it is better to find out while you are still on the showground and can carry out a proper search. When everything is ready, *remove the shoe studs* (if you have used them), put on your pony's travelling gear and load him into the trailer. Those hacking home should leave in plenty of time to get home in daylight and without hurrying. Your pony must have time to cool off so always walk the last half-mile.

Once home, unload and undress the pony and *turn him out into the field*. After a long day, the best tonic for a tired pony is a good roll and a drink from his familiar trough. If he habitually lives out, he will be happier being put back into his field straightaway, even if it is raining. *Your* best tonic is a hot bath, a good

116

supper and the satisfaction of admiring the rosettes you and your pony have won.

## The Day After

This is a day of rest. Catch up your pony and check him over carefully for any signs of tenderness or swelling in his legs. Forget about exercise and practice for one day – that can start again tomorrow. After all, both of you deserve a day off!

# Useful Addresses

**The Pony Club**

If you do not know the name and address of the secretary of your local branch, write to:

Pony Club Headquarters,
British Horse Society,
British Equestrian Centre,
Stoneleigh,
Kenilworth,
Warwickshire CV8 2LR
Tel: Coventry (0203) 696697

You can also obtain a copy of the Pony Club Mounted Games Rule Book for the current year, and a list of other Pony Club publications, from this address.

**Mounted Games Association of Great Britain**

Team competitions in this association are organised on a county basis. For information on how to contact your local organiser, write to:

Mounted Games Association of Great Britain
(MGAGB),
Bunces Farm,
Runwick,
Farnham,
Surrey

## Gymkhana Equipment

Ready-made gymkhana equipment of all kinds can be
ordered from QML in Yorkshire. It would cost quite
a lot of money to equip yourself with all the items you
would need for practising from this company, but the
equipment is well-designed and very robust. They will
send you a catalogue and price list if you write to them
at:

Quarry-Mech Limited (QML),
159 Churchfield Lane,
Kexborough,
Barnsley, S75 5DU
Tel: 0226 383805